About The Author: Bryce Palmyra

Determined to leave his mark on the culinary world, Bryce is no stranger to the kitchen. He is known by his family and friends as the best teen chef in town. When asked to describe his passion for culinary arts, Bryce says that he "is a baker in the country, and cooking should be simple." His ambition to publish a cookbook centers on the idea that "the first call that goes out after a death is the call for food, yet nobody ever knows an appropriate dish to prepare." As depressing as it sounds, every kitchen needs a go-to guide dedicated to funeral food. "Because people struggle in deciding what to cook for the grieving family," Bryce says, "this book serves as a helpful guide full of ideas that can be prepared 'in a pinch.' These are definitely the things to bring my family when I die."

Things to Bring My Family When I Die

A Go-To Guide for the
Southern Chef

Written by
15-year-old
Bryce Palmyra

ISBN: 978-1-935256-52-6

L'Edge Press
PO Box 1652
Boone, NC 28607
ledgepress@gmail.com

A portion of proceeds from this book will be donated to Hope Makes a Difference, delivering life and hope to nations around the world.

~ Dear Aunt Sadie's Popcorn Salad ~

We all have that one kooky relative who is slightly out of the ordinary. For me, that person would be my dear Aunt Sadie. She had a recipe for Popcorn Salad, and let me tell you, it was like no other. Sadie gave me this recipe just before she passed away at the early age of 77- after suffering a heart attack. Her final wish was for this recipe (which was her all-time favorite) to be at the very beginning of my cookbook. Despite the fact that many people viewed her as an awful cook, I felt it necessary to fulfill her last request. Please know that I do not endorse the following recipe in any way, and although I took it to her funeral and said it was made by my uncle Clem, I do not recommend you ever trying it yourself. I don't know if it had to do with the vicious post-funeral vomiting experienced by those who ate this salad or not, but for some reason, ever since the funeral, everyone who ate this now hates Uncle Clem…

6 cups popcorn, popped
2 cups carrots, chopped fine
2 cups celery, diced
2 cups green onions, chopped
2 cups canned water chestnuts, drained and chopped
2 pounds bacon, cooked and crumbled (reserve grease)
2 cups cheddar cheese, shredded
1/4 cup white vinegar
2 cups mayonnaise
1/2 cup lard
1 cup sugar

In a large mixing bowl, combine the popcorn, carrots, celery, green onion, water chestnuts, bacon, and cheddar cheese.

In a small bowl, combine the vinegar, reserved bacon grease, mayonnaise, lard, and sugar. Whisk well and pour over popcorn mixture.

Refrigerate overnight, or at least 5 hours to allow popcorn to break down.

Breads…

~ Applesauce Breakfast Muffins ~

1 cup (2 sticks) butter, lightly softened
1 + 1/2 cups sugar
2 eggs, lightly beaten
2 cups unsweetened applesauce
2 tbsp. baking soda
2 cups all-purpose flour, sifted
2 tbsp. cinnamon
1 + 1/2 tsp. allspice
2 tbsp. vanilla

Preheat oven to 350F. Lightly grease muffin tins; set aside.

In a large mixing bowl, cream butter and sugar until light and fluffy. Mix in beaten eggs.

Heat applesauce in a small saucepan until hot, do not boil. Stir in baking soda. (Note that baking soda will cause applesauce to bubble temporarily). Allow to cool slightly.

Pour applesauce mixture into creamed butter. Mix well. Gradually mix in sifted flour, spices, and vanilla into cream mixture. (Note that batter will be extremely thick. Also note that batter can be stored in refrigerator for up to two weeks for later use.)

Divide batter equally amongst muffin tins. Bake for 20 minutes, or until a toothpick inserted into the center of muffins comes out clean.

~ Banana and Cranberry Bread ~

1 cup sugar
2/3 cup vegetable shortening
3 eggs, beaten
3 + 1/2 cups self-rising flour, sifted
1 cup pecans, chopped
1/4 tsp. baking soda
2 cups (about 4) bananas, mashed
1 (16 ounce) can whole-berry cranberry sauce

Preheat oven to 325F. Grease and flour a 12-cup Bundt pan; set aside.

In the bowl of an electric mixer, cream sugar and shortening over medium speed until soft and fluffy. Add eggs, one at a time, beating well after each addition. Gradually add in flour, pecans, baking soda, and bananas. Continue to mix for about 1 minute until all ingredients are thoroughly combined. Stir in cranberry sauce.

Pour batter into prepared pan. Bake for 1 hour 10 minutes to 1 hour 15 minutes, or until a toothpick inserted into the center of bread comes out clean. Allow bread to rest in pan for 10 minutes. Remove bread from pan and allow bread to cool completely on a wire rack before slicing.

~ Cast-Iron Cornbread ~

2 tbsp. vegetable oil
2 cups yellow cornmeal
1 tsp. salt
1 tbsp. sugar
2 tsp. baking powder
1/2 tsp. baking soda
1 cup buttermilk
2 eggs
1 + 1/2 cups creamed corn

Preheat oven to 425F.

Grease the bottom and up the sides of a 10-inch cast-iron skillet with vegetable oil. Place skillet in preheated oven for 8 minutes while you prepare batter.

In a large mixing bowl combine remaining ingredients. Mix thoroughly until batter is smooth. Pour into hot skillet and bake for 18 to 20 minutes, or until a toothpick inserted into the center of the bread comes out clean.

~ Country Cornbread Puddin' ~

1 can whole kernel yellow corn, do not drain
1 (14 ounce) can cream-style corn
1 (8 oz.) carton sour cream
2 eggs, beaten
1 box Jiffy corn muffin mix
1 stick butter, melted

Preheat oven to 350F.

In a large bowl, combine all ingredients and mix until batter is smooth. Pour into a greased 13x9" baking dish and bake for 55 to 60 minutes, or until a toothpick inserted into the center of the pudding comes out clean.

~ Dinner Muffins ~

1 egg, beaten
1 cup milk
1/3 cup vegetable oil
2 cups all-purpose flour
1 tbsp. baking powder
1 tsp. salt
1/3 cup sugar

Preheat oven to 400F. Grease a 12-cup muffin pan; set aside.

In a medium sized mixing bowl whisk together the egg, milk, and oil. Gradually whisk in flour, baking powder, salt, and sugar.

Divide batter equally amongst muffin pan. Bake for 20-25 minutes or until a toothpick inserted into center of muffins comes out clean.

~ Farmhouse Muffins ~

1 tube (approximately 10) prepared buttermilk biscuits, uncooked
1 pound ground hamburger
1/2 cup ketchup
3 tbsp. brown sugar
1 tbsp. apple cider vinegar
1 tsp. chili powder
1 cup cheddar cheese, shredded

Preheat oven to 375F.

Divide prepared dough into 10 biscuits. Press dough into the bottom and up the sides of greased muffin tins; set aside.

In a medium frying pan brown the ground beef over medium-high heat; drain excess grease from pan and set aside.

In a small mixing bowl whisk together ketchup, brown sugar, apple cider vinegar, and chili powder until smooth. Stir in cooked hamburger meat. Divide meat mixture amongst biscuits, using about 1/4 cup for each. Sprinkle cheddar cheese over each biscuit.

Bake for 18-20 minutes, or until cheese is golden brown. Cool in pan for 5 minutes before serving.

~ Portuguese Sweet Bread ~

1 cup warm water
1 package active dry yeast
2 + 1/2 cups sugar, divided
13 cups all-purpose flour, divided
1/2 cup vegetable shortening
1 cup mashed potatoes
5 eggs, beaten

2 cups milk
1/2 cup (1 stick) butter, melted
1 tbsp. lemon extract
1/2 tsp. salt
1/2 tsp. baking soda
2 cups raisins
1 cup golden raisins

In a large mixing bowl, combine warm water, yeast, and 1 cup of sugar and allow to proof. (Yeast is proofed when water becomes frothy.) Mix in 1 cup of flour, shortening, and mashed potatoes. Cover bowl with dampened towels. Place bowl in a slightly heated oven (about 100F.) and allow dough to rise for 1 hour. Gradually mix in remaining 12 cups flour, 1 + 1/2 cups sugar, eggs, milk, butter, lemon extract, salt, baking soda, and raisins. Replace slightly dampened towel over bowl and allow to rise for an additional 1.5 hours, or until dough has doubled in size.

Grease several 9x5" loaf pans; set aside. Divide dough into approximately 6 loaves, place in prepared pans. Allow to rise in pans for an additional 45 minutes. In the meantime, allow oven to preheat to 350F. Bake for 25- 30 minutes, or until loaves are golden brown on top. Allow loaves to rest in pans for 10 minutes before transferring to wire racks to cool completely.

~ Southern Skillet Bread ~

2 tbsp. + 1/3 cup vegetable oil, divided
2 cups self-rising flour
1 cup buttermilk

Preheat oven to 450F.

Grease the bottom and up the sides of an 8" cast iron skillet with two tablespoons oil. Place in oven to heat oil for about 8 minutes while you prepare batter.

In a medium mixing bowl, combine 1/3 cup vegetable oil, flour, and buttermilk. Blend until a thick batter is formed. Stir in excess oil from hot skillet.

Pour batter into hot skillet and bake for 23-28 minutes, or until a toothpick inserted into the center of bread comes out clean.

~ Yeast Bread ~

2 + 1/4 cup warm water
2 packages active dry yeast
2 tbsp. sugar, divided
7.5 – 8 cups bread flour, divided
3 beaten eggs, divided
2 tsp. salt
1/2 cup (1 stick) butter, softened
1/2 cup sugar

    Combine water, yeast, and 1 tablespoon of sugar. Let stand for 2 minutes to allow yeast to proof. (Yeast is proofed when water begins to turn frothy). Stir in 2 cups flour; let stand for 20 minutes. Stir in 2 eggs, salt, butter, sugar and an additional 2 cups of flour. Mix until dough is smooth. Continue to add flour to make a soft dough. Transfer dough onto lightly floured workspace. Knead for 8-10 minutes, adding remaining flour, if needed, to until dough becomes very soft and elastic. Place dough in a large greased bowl and allow to rise in a warm oven (about 100F.) for approximately 1.5 – 2 hours, or until dough has doubled in size.

    Preheat oven to 350F. Divide into 4 large loaves. Place greased 9x4 loaf pans and bake for 25 to 30 minutes or until each loaf is golden brown on top. Allow to cool in pans before slicing.

Main Dishes…

The southern tradition is the minute you receive a call that some- one has died, you hang up the phone and start cooking for the grieving family. It's ill-mannered for the local community to not provide at least a week worth of comfort food. When my cousin Curtis died, there was no short of ten gallons of mashed potatoes and seventy-five pounds of fried chicken delivered to our door, and I think about three hundred seventy-nine people passed through to grieve with us. I washed no short of four hundred twen- ty-two plates that week, not counting the silverware and cups. I promised myself that I would make it federal law that a disposable plate and silverware committee be assigned after any death in the southern states, because washing four hundred twenty-two plates is far from practical.

~ Cajun Pork Roast ~

2 lb. boneless pork loin roast
4 tsp. cumin
1 tbsp. garlic powder
1/2 tsp. ground cayenne pepper
2 tsp. salt
1 tsp. black pepper
2 tbsp. vegetable oil

Preheat oven to 375F.

In a small bowl, combine all 5 spices and stir to combine. Set aside.

Place pork roast on a sheet pan and pat dry with paper towels. Rub all sides of roast with spices. Allow to rest for 30 minutes.

Heat vegetable oil in a 10-inch cast-iron skillet set to high heat. Sear pork for two minutes on each side. Transfer skillet to oven and bake for 45 minutes, or until cooked through and juices run clear.

~ Country Cabbage Rolls ~

1 egg, beaten
1 tsp. salt
1/4 tsp. pepper
2 tsp. Worcestershire Sauce
1/3 cup onion, finely chopped
2/3 cup milk
1/2 lb. ground hamburger

1/2 lb. ground turkey
1 cup rice, cooked
6 large cabbage leaves
2 (8 ounce) cans tomato sauce
1 tbsp. brown sugar
1 tbsp. lemon juice

Preheat oven to 350F.

In a medium mixing bowl combine egg, salt, pepper, Worcestershire sauce, onion, and milk, stirring until ingredients are thoroughly combined. Blend in ground beef, turkey, and rice.

Bring 6 cups water to a boil. Immerse cabbage leaves for 2-3 minutes, or until just limp; remove from heat and drain.

Place 1/2 cup meat mixture on each leaf. Fold in sides of leaf and roll ends over meat to create a roll.

Place rolls in a 12x7.5" baking dish; set aside.

In a small mixing bowl, whisk together tomato sauce, brown sugar, and lemon juice. Pour over cabbage rolls. Bake for 75-80 minutes.

~ Creamy Chicken Tetrazzini ~

1 (8-ounce) package spaghetti, broken into 4-inch pieces
1 + 3/4 cups grated Cheddar cheese, divided
4 tbsp. grated Parmesan cheese, divided
3 cups cooked chicken, chopped
1 green pepper, diced fine
1/2 medium onion, chopped
2/3 cup mushrooms, chopped
1/2 cup carrots, shredded
1 (10.5 ounce) can cream of mushroom soup
3/4 cup chicken broth (or 1/2 cup chicken broth and 1/4 cup Dry Vermouth)
1 + 1/2 tsp. salt
1 tsp. ground black pepper

Preheat oven to 350F.
Cook and drain spaghetti. Set aside.
In a large mixing bowl combine 1 + 1/4 cups Cheddar cheese, 2 tbsp. Parmesan cheese, and all remaining ingredients. Stir in cooked spaghetti.
Spread mixture into a greased 13x9" baking dish. Sprinkle with remaining cheeses.
Cover with aluminum foil and bake for 40 minutes. Remove aluminum foil and bake for an additional 5-8 minutes to allow cheese to brown.

~ Dutch Chicken with Potatoes ~

1/4 cup + 2 tbsp. all-purpose flour, divided
3/4 tsp. salt
2 tsp. paprika
2 tbsp. butter
1.5 pounds uncooked boneless chicken breasts
1.5 pounds uncooked boneless chicken thighs
1 + 1/2 cups chicken broth
1/2 cup onion, chopped
2 cloves garlic, chopped
1 lb. (about 4 small) potatoes (cut into quarter and lightly salted)
1/4 cup cold water
3 Tbsp. Dry Sherry
ground black pepper, to taste

In a small mixing bowl combine 1/4 cup flour, salt, and paprika; set aside.

Melt butter in a large skillet over medium-high heat. Coat chicken in flour, and cook in pan for 10-15 minutes, or until chicken is browned on both sides. Add chicken broth, onion, garlic, and potatoes. Reduce heat and simmer for 25-30 minutes or until tender. Remove chicken and vegetables, leaving juices reserved in pan.

In a small mixing bowl, blend together 2 Tbsp. flour with 1/4 cup cold water. Whisk into reserved juices. Cook over medium heat until mixture bubbles, whisking constantly. Whisk in dry sherry and a dash of pepper, continue to cook for an additional minute.

~ Italian Pot Roast ~

3-4 pounds Chuck or Sirloin Tip roast
2 tbsp. olive oil
1/4 cup vinegar
1 tsp. sugar
1 (8-ounce) can tomato sauce
1 tsp. salt
1 tsp. Worcestershire sauce
1/4 tsp. ground black pepper
2 tsp. Italian seasoning
2 cups whole baby carrots
1 cup mushrooms, chopped
2 medium yellow onions, quartered
4 cups white rice, cooked according to package directions (if desired)

In small mixing bowl, combine vinegar, sugar, tomato sauce, salt, Worcestershire, black pepper, and Italian seasonings. Whisk well; set aside.

Heat Olive Oil over medium-high heat in the bottom of a Dutch oven. Brown meat on all sides. Dump in carrots and mushrooms. Pour in tomato sauce mixture.

Reduce heat and simmer for 3 – 3.5 hours, or until roast is tender. Serve over rice, if desired.

~ "Mac N' Cheese" with Tomato ~

2 tsp. salt
1 pound elbow macaroni
4 + 1/2 cups milk
1 stick unsalted butter
1/2 cup all-purpose flour
4 cups mozzarella cheese, grated
3 cups mild Cheddar cheese, grated

3/4 tsp. garlic powder
3/4 tsp. ground nutmeg
3/4 tsp. black pepper
3/4 tsp. salt
3 large tomatoes, peeled and thickly sliced
2 cups Panko bread crumbs

Preheat oven to 375F.

Fill a large pot 2/3 full of water and bring to a boil. Stir in salt and macaroni. Cook for duration specified on package. Drain and set aside.

In a medium skillet heated on high, melt butter and whisk in flour. Cook for 1 minute, whisking constantly. Pour in milk, bring to a boil and continue to whisk constantly until smooth. Reduce heat to medium-low and gradually whisk in cheese, whisking constantly until cheese is melted. Remove from heat. Whisk in garlic powder, nutmeg, salt, and black pepper.

Dump cooked macaroni into a greased 13x9" pan. Pour over cheese mixture and stir until combined. Cover with sliced tomatoes.

Bake for 20 minutes. Remove from oven and sprinkle over Panko bread crumbs. Bake for 15 additional minutes until breadcrumbs are golden brown.

Remove from oven and allow to cool slightly before serving.

~ Mighty Meatloaf ~

2 lbs. ground hamburger
1 + 1/2 cups shredded cheddar cheese (divided)
2 cups Italian bread crumbs
1 egg, beaten
1/2 cup celery, chopped
1/2 cup onion, chopped
1/2 cup carrot, chopped
2 tsp. Worcestershire sauce
1 tsp. salt
1 tsp pepper
1 (8 ounce) can tomato sauce
1 tbsp. sugar

Preheat oven to 350F.

In a large mixing bowl, combine ground sirloin, 1 cup cheese, breadcrumbs, beaten egg, celery, onion, carrots, Worcestershire sauce, salt, and pepper. Mix well. Shape into a ball and place onto a 9x9" baking dish. Bake for 1 hour.

In a small bowl, combine tomato sauce and sugar and pour over meatloaf. Sprinkle with remaining 1/2 cup of cheddar cheese. Bake an additional 15 minutes.

~ "Sauce-less" Spaghetti with Meatballs ~

2 tbsp. olive oil
5 large tomatoes, chopped
1 large onion, chopped
1 cup mushrooms, thickly sliced
2 slices sandwich bread
1/2 cup water
1 lb. ground hamburger
2 eggs, lightly beaten

1 tbsp. dried parsley
2 tsp. dried basil, divided
1 tsp. dried oregano, divided
3/4 tsp. salt, divided
1/3 + 1/4 tsp. black pepper, divided
1 (16-ounce) package spaghetti,
   cooked according to package directions

Heat oil in a large, non-stick skillet over medium-high heat. Stir in tomatoes, onion, and mushrooms. Cover, reduce heat to medium, stirring occasionally until vegetables begin to release their juices (about 3 minutes). Season with 1 tsp. basil, 1/2 tsp. oregano, 1/2 tsp. salt, and 1/3 tsp. pepper. Add 1/3 cup water. Cover and reduce heat to low.

Place bread in a small bowl. Cover with 1/2 cup water. Allow to sit for 2 minutes. Drain and set aside. In a medium mixing bowl combine hamburger, eggs, soaked bread, parsley, remaining 1 tsp. basil, 1/2 tsp. oregano, 1/4 tsp. salt, and 1/4 tsp pepper. Stir until ingredients are thoroughly combined. Drop by tablespoon-sized balls into pan. Increase heat to medium-high, replace lid, and allow to cook for 8 to 10 minutes, or until meat is cooked through, turning halfway through. Serve over cooked pasta.

- Savory Tomato Pie -

1 prepared pie shell (homemade or store bought both work fine)
1 medium onion, diced
4 large tomatoes (peeled, seeded, and thickly sliced)
1 cup mayonnaise
1 + 1/2 cups cheddar cheese, shredded
1/2 cup parmesan cheese, shredded
1/2 tsp. dried oregano
2 tsp. dried basil
1/2 tsp. salt
1/2 tsp. black pepper

Preheat oven to 375F. Press pie crust into the bottom and up the sides of a 9" pie pan. Bake for 7 minutes. Remove from oven; set aside to cool.

In a medium mixing bowl, combine mayonnaise, cheddar cheese, parmesan cheese, oregano, basil, salt, and pepper. Stir well to combine.

Layer tomatoes and diced onions in partially cooked pie shell. Spread cheese mixture evenly atop tomatoes.

Bake for 30-35 minutes, or until cheese mixture is golden brown. Remove from oven and allow to rest on counter for 10-15 minutes before slicing.

~ Summer Squash Breakfast Casserole ~

1 lb. ground hamburger
5 tbsp. all-purpose flour, divided
2 tbsp. butter
3 cups zucchini, sliced
3 cups yellow squash, sliced
1/2 cup onion, chopped

1 3/4 cup cottage cheese
1/4 cup parmesan cheese, shredded
2 eggs, beaten
1 tsp. garlic salt
1 cup Cheddar cheese, shredded

Preheat oven to 350F.

Brown meat in a medium sized skillet; drain grease. Toss meat in 2 tbsp. flour and spread into bottom of 13x9" baking dish.

In a medium frying pan, melt butter over medium heat. Sauté zucchini, squash, and onion until tender. Toss in remaining 3 tbsp. flour. Pour 4 cups of the squash mixture over hamburger and set aside.

In a medium mixing bowl combine cottage cheese, parmesan cheese, eggs, and garlic salt. Spread atop squash mixture. Spread remaining amount of squash mixture over cheese blend.

Bake for 30 minutes. Remove from oven and sprinkle remaining 1 cup Cheddar cheese over casserole. Bake for an additional 5 minutes, or until cheese is melted.

Side Dishes...

Sometimes life throws publically humiliating circumstances at us. Sometimes such circumstances occur during bad times. Sometimes the bad time is during a funeral. The funeral was for my friend's grandma. Trudy passed away at the age of one-hundred two. She lived a heroic life, and her grandson, forty-seven-year-old Coleman, was assigned to the eulogy. He gave a stunning speech, and as he walked off stage his life took a turn for the worse…Coleman's pants tumbled to the ground. Laughter billowed from every seat, and seeing the director was at a complete loss for words, the service ended abruptly.

~ Black-Eyed-Pea Salad with Vegetables ~

1 can black eyed peas, rinsed and drained
1 can chickpeas, rinsed and drained
2 bell peppers, chopped
2 large tomatoes, chopped
3 tbsp. green onion, chopped
2 avocados, chopped
2/3 cup Italian salad dressing

Combine all ingredients in a large mixing bowl. Refrigerate for 3 to 5 hours before serving.

~ Potatoes "Au Gratin" ~

5 russet potatoes, peeled and sliced
1 onion, chopped thick
3/4 tsp. salt
3/4 tsp. pepper
3 tbsp. butter
3 tbsp. all-purpose flour
1/2 tsp. salt
2 cups milk
2 cups mild Cheddar cheese, shredded

Preheat oven to 400F.

Layer 1/2 of the potatoes into bottom of a greased 9x9" baking dish. Cover with chopped onions, and cover with remaining potatoes. Sprinkle with salt and pepper.

In a medium-sized saucepan set over medium heat, melt butter. Whisk in flour and salt, and continue to whisk constantly for one minute. Whisk in milk. Increase heat to high and continue whisking constantly until mixture has thickened. Remove from heat. Whisk in cheese, and continue whisking until melted. Pour cheese sauce over potatoes. Cover with aluminum foil.

Bake 70 minutes. Remove aluminum foil and bake for an additional 15 minutes. Remove from oven and allow to cool slightly before serving.

~ Citrus Rice Salad with Asparagus ~

1 (14.5 ounces) can chicken broth
1 cup white rice
1/3 cup water
1/2 cup fresh asparagus, cut into 1-inch pieces
1 cup frozen peas
2 tbsp. green onions, sliced fine
1/4 cup olive oil
4 tbsp. lemon juice
3 tbsp. sour cream
1 tsp. lemon zest
1/2 tsp. salt
1/4 tsp. black pepper

Bring chicken broth to a boil in a pot set to high heat. Stir in rice. Reduce heat, cover and simmer for 15 – 18 minutes or until all broth is absorbed by rice. Remove from heat.

Bring water to boil in a medium saucepan set to high heat. Stir in asparagus and peas. Return to boil and cook until tender, approximately 3 – 5 minutes. Remove from heat and drain.

Combine rice, asparagus, peas, and green onions. Set aside.

In a small bowl, whisk together remaining ingredients. Pour over rice. Serve immediately.

~ Cold Lentil Salad ~

5 slices bacon
1 cup carrots, chopped fine
5 cloves garlic, chopped coarse
1 medium red pepper, chopped
1 medium onion, chopped
6 cups chicken broth
2 cups dried lentils

2/3 cup tomatoes, chopped
4 tsp. olive oil
3/4 tsp. salt
3/4 tsp. black pepper
2 tsp. garlic powder
4 tsp. dried parsley

Cook bacon in a large pot over medium heat until crispy. Remove bacon and allow to cool before crumbling into pieces.

Add carrots, garlic, red pepper, and onion to pot and cook over medium-high heat for 3 minutes, stirring often.

Pour chicken broth and lentils into pot. Increase heat to high and bring to a boil. Reduce heat to medium-low. Cover and allow to cook over a heavy simmer for 30 minutes. Add spices and continue to simmer for approximately 5 minutes or until all liquid is absorbed. Stir in bacon crumbles. Remove from heat.

Once cool, place in refrigerator until cold and serve.

~ Cornbread Salad ~

1 pan cornbread, cubed (recipe can be found on page 11)
1 can kidney beans
1 can corn, drained and rinsed
2 large tomatoes, chopped
1 large bell pepper, chopped
1 medium onion, chopped
1 large cucumber, chopped
1 cup sour cream
1 cup mayonnaise
1 packet ranch dressing mix
2 cups mild cheddar cheese, grated

In medium mixing bowl, combine beans, corn, tomatoes, bell pepper, onion, and cucumber. Set aside.

In a small mixing bowl, whisk together sour cream, mayonnaise, and ranch dressing mix. Set aside.

In a large trifle dish, layer half of the cornbread, vegetables, dressing, and cheese. Repeat layers. Refrigerate overnight before serving.

~ Green Bean Casserole ~

1/2 stick butter
1/2 cup onion, chopped
3/4 cup mushrooms, chopped
3 cups green beans, cut into 1-inch pieces
4 cups chicken broth
1 (10-ounce) can cream of mushroom soup
1 tsp. garlic powder
3/4 tsp. salt
3/4 tsp. black pepper
1 (3-ounce) can French-fried onion rings
1 cup mild Cheddar cheese, grated

Preheat oven to 350F.

In a medium skillet, melt butter and sauté onions and mushrooms for about 4 minutes, or until just vegetables are just slightly crunchy. Set aside.

In a medium pot, bring chicken broth to a boil and cook beans for 5 minutes. Drain and set aside.

In a large mixing bowl, combine cooked onions, mushrooms, green beans, cream of mushroom soup, garlic powder, salt, and pepper.

Pour mixture into a greased 13x9" baking dish. Bake for 20 minutes. Remove from oven and sprinkle with onion rings and cheddar cheese. Bake for 10 additional minutes to melt cheese. Remove from oven and allow to cool for 5 minutes before serving.

~ Green Beans with Herb Glaze ~

4 cups uncooked green beans
7 cloves garlic, sliced thick
3 tbsp. olive oil
2 tsp. dried basil
3/4 tsp. dried oregano
3/4 tsp. salt
3/4 tsp. black pepper

Steam green beans and garlic for 7 – 10 minutes or until just tender. Remove from heat and place in a serving dish.

In a small mixing bowl whisk together olive oil, basil, oregano, salt, and pepper. Pour over green beans and garlic. Serve immediately.

~ "Perfect" Pasta Salad ~

1 (1-Lb.) box macaroni
1 (8-ounce) block cheddar cheese, cubed
1 medium jar green olives with pimentos, drained and chopped
1 small can black olives, drained and sliced
1 medium white onion, chopped
1 large tomato, chopped
1 cup cucumber, chopped
1/3 cup mayonnaise
1 tsp. garlic powder
3/4 tsp. salt
3/4 tsp. black pepper

Cook pasta according to package directions. Drain and allow to cool.
In a large mixing bowl, combine pasta, cheddar cheese, olives and pimentos, onion, tomato, cucumber, mayonnaise, salt, and pepper. Refrigerate overnight.
Add additional mayonnaise and seasoning prior to serving, if desired.

~ Summer Salad with Cider Vinaigrette ~

5 cups spinach
5 tbsp. green onion, chopped fine
1/2 cup mushrooms, sliced
5 pieces bacon, cooked and crumbled
1/4 cup maple syrup
3 tbsp. apple cider vinegar
2 tbsp. canola oil
1/4 tsp. salt
1/4 tsp. pepper
1/2 tsp. garlic powder

Combine first four ingredients in a serving dish.

In a small mixing bowl, whisk together remaining ingredients until thoroughly combined. Pour over spinach mixture. Keep in refrigerator up to a day until ready to serve.

~ Sweet Potato with "Mallow" ~

1 (40-ounce) can cut yams, drained
3/4 cup golden raisins
3/4 cup brown sugar
1/3 tsp. salt
2 tsp. cinnamon
1/4 tsp. all-spice
1 egg, beaten
1/2 stick butter, melted
1 (16-ounce) bag miniature marshmallows, divided

Preheat oven to 350F.

In a large mixing bowl, mash yams. Stir in golden raisins, brown sugar, salt, cinnamon, all-spice, egg, and butter.

Spread half of mixture into a greased 13x9" baking dish, top with half of marshmallows, and cover with remaining sweet potato mixture.

Bake for 30 minutes. Remove from oven and top with remaining half of marshmallows. Bake for 10 additional minutes. Remove from oven and allow to cool slightly before serving.

Desserts...

While my aunt was visiting the iconic state of Illinois in the 1980's due the the death of her dear friend Gertrude, she found herself completely dumbfounded that the family had the corpse displayed in a casket centered in their living room...And she stayed displayed for two days prior to the funeral. This did not affect any small children or relatives in the house, as they continued to live life as usual – talking, playing, and of course eating...Seventeen gallons of banana pudding were consumed while admiring Gertrude for the final time.

~ Autumn Apple Cheesecake ~

1 cup graham cracker, crumbled
1 cup sugar, divided
1 tsp. cinnamon, divided
3 tbsp. butter, melted
2 (8-ounce) packages cream cheese, softened
2 eggs
1/2 tsp. vanilla
4 cups apples, peeled and thinly sliced
1/2 cup pecans, chopped

Preheat oven to 350F.

Combine graham cracker crumbs, 3 tablespoons sugar, ½ teaspoon of the cinnamon and the butter. Press into the bottom and up the sides of a 9-inch pie pan. Bake 10 minutes. Remove from oven and allow to cool.

Beat together cream cheese and ½ cup sugar in large bowl or mixer until well blended. Add eggs, one at a time, beating well after each addition. Blend in vanilla; pour into cooled crust.

Combine 1/3 cup sugar and the remaining ½ teaspoon cinnamon in a small bowl. Pour over apples and toss to combine. Spoon over cream cheese mixture; sprinkle with pecans. Bake for 70 minutes, or until set. Allow to cool; refrigerate overnight. Do not remove from pie pan.

~ Banana Pudding with Meringue ~

2 (3-ounce) packages vanilla pudding mix
4 + 1/2 cups milk
3 eggs yolks
3 large bananas, sliced
6 ounces vanilla wafers
dash of cream of tartar
3 egg whites, separated
1/3 cup sugar

Preheat oven to 350°F.

In a medium sized saucepan set to medium heat, whisk together pudding mix, milk, and egg yolks. Bring to a heavy boil and allow to cook for 2 minutes, whisking constantly. Remove from heat and allow to cool. Stir in banana slices.

In the bottom of a 2-quart baking dish, layer half of the vanilla wafers and top with half of the pudding mixture. Repeat layers. Set aside.

In the bowl of an electric mixer, beat egg whites and cream of tartar on medium speed until foamy. Gradually pour in sugar, increase speed to medium-high, and continue to mix until stiff peaks form. Spread over pudding.

Bake for 15 minutes until meringue is browned. Remove from oven and allow to cool completely. Refrigerate for a couple hours to chill before serving.

~ Chocolate Chewy Cake Bars ~

1 stick butter
1 (1 lb.) box brown sugar
2 eggs, beaten
1 tsp. vanilla extract
2 cups self-rising flour
1 cup pecans, chopped
1 cup semi-sweet chocolate chips

Preheat oven to 350F. Grease a 13x9" baking dish; set aside.

In a small saucepan over medium heat, melt butter and brown sugar; remove from heat. In in medium mixing bowl combine eggs, vanilla, and butter mixture. Mix well. Gradually mix in flour. Stir in pecans and chocolate chips.

Spread batter into prepared baking dish. Bake for about 30 minutes, or until golden brown on top.

~ Chocolate Torte ~

1 package chocolate wafer,
   crumbled in food processor
1 stick butter, melted
1 bag semi-sweet chocolate chips,
   melted in microwave
2 cups heavy whipping cream (Do
   not substitute)

6 egg yolks, beaten
2 tsp. vanilla
5 1/2 cups confectioners' sugar
1/2 cup cocoa
1/2 cup butter, softened
2 tsp. vanilla
milk (as needed to achieve desired thickness)

Preheat oven to 350F. Grease a 9" round spring form pan with butter, set aside.

In a medium-sized mixing bowl combine the crumbled wafers and butter. Press into the bottom and 2 inches up the sides of the greased spring-form pan. Place spring-form on a cookie sheet and bake for 10 minutes. Remove from oven. Set aside and allow to cool completely.

In a medium-sized mixing bowl whisk together the heavy whipping cream, eggs, and vanilla. Gradually whisk the cream mixture into the melted chocolate and keep whisking for approximately one minute, or until smooth. Pour into crust and bake for 45-50 minutes, or until cracks have formed around edges of custard. Remove from oven and allow to cool for 2 hours.

In the bowl of a standing mixer, beat butter and vanilla until creamy. Gradually add in the cocoa and confectioners' sugar and beat on medium just until fully incorporated, scraping down sides of bowl with a rubber spatula as needed. Add milk as needed to achieve desired thickness. Spread frosting atop cake. Cover and refrigerate for six hours, or preferably overnight. Allow to sit at room temperature for 30 minutes prior to serving. For best results, run a knife around the edge of the spring-form pan just prior to cutting.

~ Devil's Food Cake with Vanilla ~

2.5 cups all-purpose flour
2 tsp. baking soda
1/2 tsp. salt
1/2 cup cocoa
2 cups sugar
1 stick butter, softened
1/2 cup shortening
2 tsp. vanilla
2 eggs

1 cup buttermilk
1 cup boiling water

1 stick butter, softened
3/4 cup shortening
2 tsp. vanilla
6 cups powdered sugar
milk, amount needed will vary depending
    on desired thickness

Preheat oven to 325F.

In a medium mixing bowl, combine flour, soda, salt, and cocoa. Mix until thoroughly combined.

In the bowl of a standing electric mixer, cream butter and shortening. Add sugar, vanilla, eggs, and buttermilk. Blend until combined. Slowly add in flour mixture, and blend until smooth. Stir in boiling water.

Pour mixture into a greased 13x9" metal baking pan. Bake for 28 minutes, or until a toothpick inserted into the center of the cake comes out clean. Allow to cool completely before preparing frosting.

For the frosting:

In the bowl of a standing electric mixer, cream butter, shortening, and vanilla. With the mixer set to low, slowly add powdered sugar. Blend in milk, 1 tablespoon at a time, until desired thickness is reached. Spread frosting on prepared cake.

~ Peach Cobbler ~

2 cups self-rising flour
1 + 1/2 cups sugar
2 cups milk, at room temperature
1 + 1/2 sticks butter, melted
2 (15 ounce) cans sliced peaches in syrup, do not drain

Preheat oven to 350F.

In a medium mixing bowl, combine flour, sugar, milk, and melted butter. Mix thoroughly. Spread into the bottom of a greased 13x9" baking dish. Pour peaches over flour mixture. Sprinkle with cinnamon.

Bake for 35-40 minutes. Remove from oven and allow to cool for 10 minutes before serving.

~ Summer Strawberry Cake ~

1 box white cake mix
1 box strawberry Jell-O
4 eggs, beaten
2/3 cup vegetable oil
1/2 cup water
1/2 cup strawberries, chopped
2 tsp. lemon juice
2 tbsp. sugar

4 tbsp. butter, softened
8 cups powdered sugar
3/4 cup strawberries
2 tsp. lemon juice
2 tbsp. sugar

Preheat oven to 350F. Grease 13x9" sheet pan; set aside.

In a small mixing bowl, combine strawberries, lemon juice, and sugar. Stir well until sugar forms a glaze over strawberries. Place in refrigerator to allow strawberries to release their juices.

In a medium mixing bowl, whisk together cake mix, jell-o, eggs, oil, and water until thoroughly combined. Stir in strawberries and their juices. Spread batter into prepared sheet pan. Bake for 30 minutes, or until a toothpick inserted into the center of the cake comes out clean and the center is set. Allow cake to cool before preparing frosting. Do not remove cake from pan.

For the frosting:

In a small mixing bowl, combine strawberries, lemon juice, and sugar. Stir well until sugar forms a glaze over strawberries. Place in refrigerator to allow strawberries to release their juices.

In the bowl of a standing mixer, cream butter and powdered sugar over medium-low speed. Gradually mix in strawberries and their juices. Continue to blend until frosting is smooth and creamy. Spread over prepared cake.

~ Index ~

~ Index ~

www.ingramcontent.com/pod-product-compliance
Lightning Source LLC
Chambersburg PA
CBHW061412090426
42741CB00022B/3488